The World of Mythology:
Native American Mythology

By Jim Ollhoff

VISIT US AT
WWW.ABDOPUBLISHING.COM

Published by ABDO Publishing Company, 8000 West 78th Street, Suite 310, Edina, MN 55439. Copyright ©2012 by Abdo Consulting Group, Inc. International copyrights reserved in all countries. No part of this book may be reproduced in any form without written permission from the publisher. ABDO & Daughters™ is a trademark and logo of ABDO Publishing Company.

Printed in the United States of America, North Mankato, Minnesota.
012011
092011

 PRINTED ON RECYCLED PAPER

Editor: John Hamilton
Graphic Design: Sue Hamilton
Cover Design: Neil Klinepier
Cover Photo: Gonzalo Ordóñez
Interior Photos and Illustrations: Aaron Paquette-pg 13; AP-pgs 7 & 17; Getty Images-pgs 5, 9, 16, 28 & 29; Glow Images-pgs 19 & 24; Granger Collection-pg 20; iStockphoto-pgs 4, 26 & borders; Library of Congress-pgs 12, 15, 22, 23, 25 & 27; National Geographic-pg 10; Samuel Edelstein-pg 21; Stacy Wiggins-pg 14; Thinkstock-pgs 8, 11, 18 & 31.

Library of Congress Cataloging-in-Publication Data

Ollhoff, Jim, 1959-
  Native American mythology / Jim Ollhoff.
    p. cm. -- (The world of mythology)
  ISBN 978-1-61714-717-3
  1. Indian mythology--North America--Juvenile literature. I. Title.
  E98.R3O44 2011
  299.7--dc22
                              2010043188

CONTENTS

THE MIGHTY MYTH

To the best of our knowledge, dogs don't wonder why or how the universe started. And we're pretty sure cows don't think about life after death. But people think about these things.

Since the beginning of time, people have told stories that help us understand life, death, and our place in the world. Stories tell us important truths about life, and help us cope with its daily challenges. These stories are called myths.

Some myths focus on gods and goddesses. Some myths talk about how the Earth got where it is, and why the stars are in the sky. Other myths focus on people and the journeys they take. Others tell stories about good personality traits, like generosity, heroism, or treating others with respect. Myths are stories that have been passed down through generations to us today.

Native American cultures, like all other cultures, passed down myths about how the world began, how life works, and how to live.

Right: Utah's Newspaper Rock is a display of Native American petroglyphs etched into stone. It shows almost 2,000 years of activity in the area.

Above: A Native American grandfather passes down stories to listening children.

NATIVE AMERICANS: 500 DIFFERENT CULTURES

Sometime between 15,000 and 30,000 years ago, and possibly earlier, people from Siberia came by land to North America.

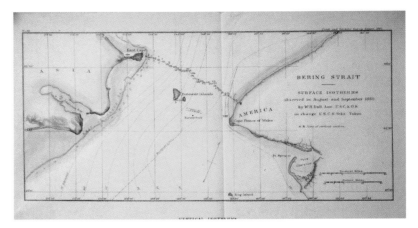

Above: A map showing where there was once an exposed land bridge between Siberia and Alaska, allowing people to cross.

Sea levels were lower at that time, exposing a land bridge between Siberia and Alaska. They also came by boat, hugging the coastline of the Americas. It's also possible that they came by boat across the South Pacific and the North Atlantic Oceans. There were probably many waves of immigrants.

These immigrants spread across the North and South American continents, forming tribal groups. By the time Europeans arrived in the late 1400s and early 1500s, there were more than 500 separate cultural groups. Christopher Columbus called the people "Indians" because he thought he had landed in India.

Above: In the 1600s, the Wampanoags of Massachusetts were the first Native Americans to meet the Pilgrims from Europe. It's estimated that up to 90 percent of the tribe's members died due to the spread of smallpox.

As European-Americans spread across North America, the Native American peoples were pushed off their ancestral lands. Much of the Native American way of life was lost to warfare, and many Native Americans were lost to European diseases such as smallpox.

In many areas, the government in the 1800s and early 1900s forbade the speaking of native languages or participating in Native American rituals. Sadly, much of Native American language, culture, and mythology have been lost.

THE SOUL OF THE NATIVE AMERICANS

At one time, there were hundreds of individual Native American tribes, each with its own mythologies. However, there are similarities between tribes in the same area. Native American tribes are sometimes grouped into five regions: the Northeast, the Southeast, the Plains (the central part of North America), the Northwest, and the Southwest.

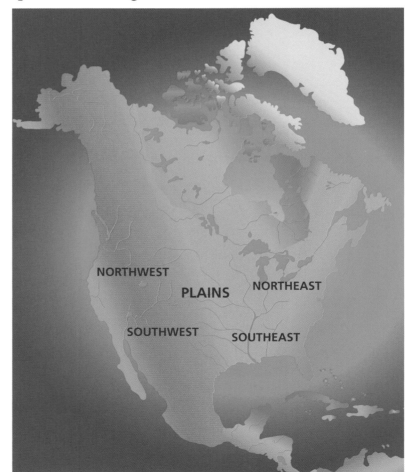

NORTHWEST

PLAINS

NORTHEAST

SOUTHWEST

SOUTHEAST

Right: Native American tribes are sometimes grouped into five general regions.

Native American mythology is deeply connected to nature. The people saw themselves in a complex web of connections with their Mother Earth. They believed humans were simply one part of nature. European-Americans bought and sold land as if it was something a person could own. This was confusing to Native Americans, who saw the land as sacred.

Left: Native Americans were a people who were deeply connected to the land and Mother Earth. Their deities controlled everything from the seasons to corn and other crops.

Since everything was connected to Mother Earth, every plant and animal had a spirit. Deities controlled the seasons, the stars, life and death, even the corn and crops. Coyotes were popular in the Southwest for their spirit power. In the Northwest, the raven was a favorite.

A Native American woman from the Northwest wears a raven headdress.

To show some of the important animal spirits, many Northwest Indians, such as those in Alaska, carved wooden totem poles. Totem poles became symbols for the tribe, and important parts of their identity.

Native American mythology paid very little thought to the afterlife. Only the "now" was important. The Plains Indians sometimes talked about a "happy hunting ground" after this life. That afterlife was very much like the current life, except there was more food available.

Left: A Tlingit tribe totem pole featuring an eagle and a salmon in Ketchican, Alaska.

COMMON THEMES IN NATIVE AMERICAN MYTHOLOGY

The hundreds of different Native American tribes all had different myths and stories. However, they had a few common themes. One of the common themes among most tribes was the idea of the

Great Spirit. The Great Spirit was usually male. He was called Osage by the Sioux tribe, or Kitchi Manitou by the Algonquian tribe of the Northeast, or Airsekui by the Huron. The Great Spirit was usually not well defined. He didn't have the personality traits of the high gods of Greek or Norse mythology.

"Appeal to the Great Spirit"

Another common theme among most tribes was the Earth Mother. The Earth, typically female, was responsible for crops. The Cherokee tribe called her Grandmother Sun. For the Southwest Hopi tribe, she was called Kokyanwuhti. Myths often said that the Earth Mother would grow old throughout the year. She started the year young in the spring, but by winter she was old. She would be reborn the next spring.

Above: Kokyanwuhti, or Spider Woman, is part of the Hopi Indians' Earth Mother myth.

Right: In some Native American myths, the world rested on the shell of a turtle.

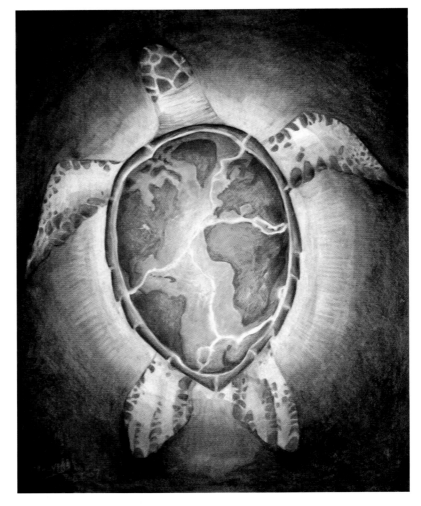

Creation stories in Native American mythology often revolved around the Earth Diver. The stories often identified an animal that dove to the bottom of the sea. It brought up special mud, and with this mud the world was created. In some myths, the world rested on the shell of a turtle.

One of the interesting themes in Native American mythology is the trickster. The trickster is a creature that is mischievous and fun, but can also be vindictive and selfish. Sometimes, the tricksters—often portrayed as a coyote or rabbit—were resourceful, but they often got themselves in trouble because of their own trickery. Tricksters are common in mythologies of the world, but they play a much larger role in Native American mythology.

A person who could communicate with the spirit world was called a shaman. The term "medicine man" usually refers not to the shaman, but to the shaman's assistant. Shamans claimed to be able to cure the sick and get important information from the spirit world. Often, a member of the tribe would receive this shamanistic power during sickness. Other times, they would receive the power during a vision quest—an alone time where the person sought the spirit world.

One account of a Northwest Kwakiutl tribe shaman says he was sick with smallpox. While he was in a fevered state, he said he saw wolves enter his hut. The wolves licked his sores and filled his body with spirit

power. The wolves told him he could now heal people and communicate with the spirit world.

Left: A Navajo shaman of the late 1800s.

NORTHEAST TRIBES

The Northeast tribes included the Iroquois Confederacy, the Huron, Delaware, and many others. They recorded their myths in strings of beads called wampum.

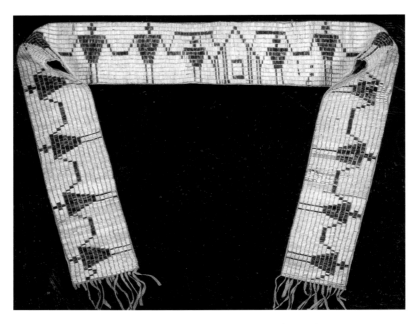

Above: A wampum belt made with strings of beads.

Some Northeast myths explained natural phenomenon. They said that brave warriors who died became the Aurora Borealis, or northern lights. They also had myths that explained the movements of the sun and the moon. The sun and moon were husband and wife. When they would quarrel, the moon got smaller and smaller. Soon, she was just a faint sliver of light. She grew back full again, but then they would quarrel and she would get small again.

Another myth explained thunder. The thunder god, Heng, would send rain that gave life to the crops. But sometimes, his children made too much noise and the weather became destructive.

Above: Some Northeast tribes' myths explained natural phenomenon. For example, the Aurora Borealis, or northern lights, were said to be brave warriors who had died.

SOUTHEAST TRIBES

Tribes in the Southeast part of North America included the Seminole, Cherokee, and Creek. One of their stories describes how people first got fire. The sky gods, who had fire, did not want to share it with humans. The rabbit thought this was terribly unfair. So, when the sky gods had a festival, the rabbit pretended to dance, and then got too close to the fire. His hair caught on fire, and he ran and ran—right down to Earth, giving fire to humans for the first time.

Above: A rabbit took fire from the sky gods and gave it to people.

Another story from the Miccosukee tribe of Florida tells how people got corn. Two brothers lived with their grandmother. They ate meat at every meal, and eventually grew tired of it. They asked for something new. She began to serve them corn, but she refused to say where she got it. So the brothers spied on her one day, and saw her rub corn off her body, like corn off a cob. The boys refused to eat the corn, and told her that they had spied on her. She told them that she would have to leave forever, but that corn would always grow from where she was buried.

Left: A Miccosukee Indian woman. According to myth, it was a grandmother who gave corn to the Miccosukee tribe.

THE PLAINS TRIBES

he Plains tribes were the Native Americans who lived in the central part of North America, where the land is mostly flat. Many of the people hunted buffalo, lived in tipis, and wore feathered headdresses. There were many Plains tribes, including the Blackfoot, Sioux, Pawnee, and Cheyenne.

Myths always spring up around important activities. In the case of the Plains Indians, one of these activities was the buffalo hunt. Buffalo were used for food and clothing. Hunting was a dangerous activity, since giant herds of running buffalo could become an unstoppable force.

A buffalo hunt on the plains.

One important myth is the story of the Buffalo Woman. Two hunters were out walking when they met a beautiful woman clothed in white buckskin. One of the men treated her rudely, and so she turned him into a pile of bones. The Buffalo Woman told the other hunter that she was going to come to his village. He returned to his tribe and told them to prepare a tipi for her. When the Buffalo Woman arrived at the village, she gave the people a sacred pipe that allowed them to communicate with the spirit world. She reminded them that all people were of the same family. As she walked away, she became a white buffalo.

Left: The Buffalo Woman story tells of a woman who gave Native Americans a sacred pipe that allowed them to communicate with the spirit world.

An important ritual for the Plains Indians was the sun dance. Communities would come together in the spring to celebrate. Young men would dance around a tall pole that symbolized the linking of Earth and sky. They danced for hours, even days, and sometimes pierced themselves. This dance was conducted so the spirits of the Earth would renew and regenerate for another year.

Right: A sun dance ritual where the young men pierce their chests and dance around a tall pole.

The vision quest was another important way to communicate with the spirit world. A person would go off to an isolated area to receive advice or enlightenment from the spirits of the land and animals. For some tribes, nearly all young males went on a vision quest as part of the transition from youth to adulthood.

A Teton Sioux Indian performing a vision quest ceremony.

SOUTHWEST TRIBES

Some of the tribes that lived in the Southwest part of North America, such as the Navajo and Apache, were nomadic, moving regularly to follow food sources. Other tribes, like the Hopi and Zuni, lived in pueblos, communities with buildings often made of stone or mud.

Most Native American tribes believed in the spirit world, and almost everything had spirits associated with it. For many of the Southwestern tribes, the spirits were called Kachinas. There might be a Kachina for a field, or a star, or animal, or almost anything. While the Kachinas were not worshipped, they could help with all kinds of things. These spirits might bring rainfall, or help with crops, or help protect travelers.

The land in the Southwest is dry, much of it desert. Many myths emerged about how to make it rain. Like many myths, these gave people the belief that they had some control over the natural world.

Right: Hopi Kachina dolls represent figures from Hopi mythology.

Above: Apaches were nomadic, moving regularly to find food.

Above: Hopis lived in stone or mud buildings called pueblos.

Other myths were simply told for fun. A Navajo myth tells about a time when bad giants covered the Earth. They ate human children, which made Coyote angry. Coyote invited a giant to take a sweat bath with him, like a modern-day sauna. Coyote told the giant he would perform a magical feat—he would break his own leg and then heal it. The giant wanted to see this trick! The sweat lodge was very dark, and so Coyote pulled out a deer leg, pretending it was his own. He broke it with a rock, and then showed it to the giant. Then he pretended to heal himself, and showed his own leg to the giant. The giant was amazed. Coyote then offered to do the same thing to the giant, and the giant agreed. Coyote smashed the giant's leg with the rock, and then ran out of the lodge.

Right: A coyote howling.

Above and Below: To protect Navajo children, the myth says Coyote tricked a bad giant into a dark sweat lodge, and smashed the giant's leg with a rock.

Northwest Tribes

The Northwest tribes included the people who inhabited the northwestern part of the United States and Canada, all the way up into Alaska. These tribes included the Tlingit, Nez Perce, Kwakiutl, Makah, and Coeur d'Alene.

Like most Native American tribes, they believed that spirits inhabited animals, fish, and plants. These spirits were called totems. The Northwest tribes often carved totems into a tall pole, which gave identity to the tribe or the community.

The Northwest tribes, like most Native American tribes, felt a closeness to the animal and plant worlds. They believed that the animals and plants provided for their food, shelter, and their very life. One myth tells this very clearly: The Wolf Clan lived in an area with many animals, and the rivers had many fish. The people of the clan became fat and lazy.

Above: An abandoned Native American village with broken totem poles on the ground.

They killed animals for sport, and left the carcasses on the ground to rot. They even jammed candles into the backs of fish, so they could see the river at night. The elders of the tribe warned them to stop, but the younger people kept wasting the lives of the animals. Then, one night, all the spirits of the animals came together and created an enormous fire and earthquake, destroying the tribe and their wicked ways.

Above: A Native American wears a wolf headdress.

GLOSSARY

CREATION MYTHS

Stories about how the world began. In Native American mythology, creation myths often revolved around the Earth Diver.

DEITY

Another name for a god or goddess.

EARTH DIVER

An animal who dives down into water and brings up mud to create the world.

GREAT SPIRIT

The main deity for most Indian tribes.

IMMIGRANTS

People who make a foreign country their home.

MEDICINE MAN

An assistant or helper to a shaman.

RITUAL

A type of religious or serious ceremony with actions that are performed in a specific order.

SACRED

Something or someone shown great respect. Usually associated with a god or religious deity.

SHAMAN

A person who could communicate with the spirit world. Often a religious leader or healer.

SMALLPOX

An often deadly disease. Europeans unknowingly brought the virus with them to the New World, where people had no immunity to it.

SWEAT LODGE

A closed hut made from sticks, mud, or animal skins and filled with steam. Native Americans used it for purification ceremonies and for healing various diseases.

TOTEM POLE

A carved pole that shows animal spirits, popular among the Northwest Indian tribes.

TRICKSTER

A common figure in mythology. It is a mischievous being, clever and frequently playing pranks on others. However, the trickster often gets into trouble because of his horseplay.

INDEX